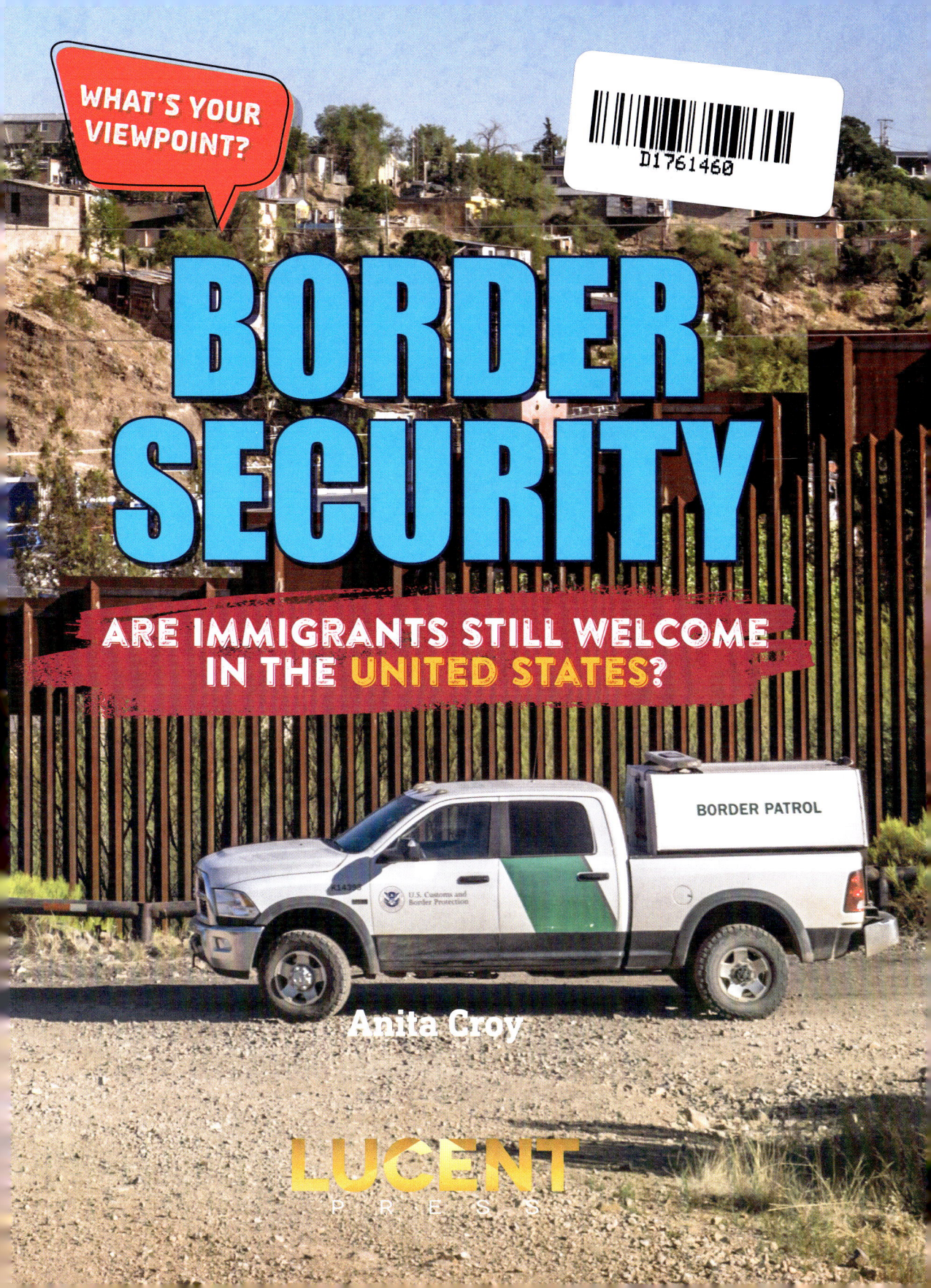

Published in 2020 by
Lucent Press, an Imprint of Greenhaven Publishing, LLC
353 3rd Avenue
Suite 255
New York, NY 10010

Copyright © 2020 Lucent Press, an Imprint of Greenhaven Publishing, LLC.

All rights reserved. No part of this book may be reproduced in any form without permission in writing from the publisher, except by a reviewer.

Produced for Lucent by Calcium
Editors: Sarah Eason and Tim Cooke
Designers: Paul Myerscough and Lynne Lennon
Picture researcher: Rachel Blount

Picture credits: Cover: Shutterstock: Manuela Durson (bg), Thomas Koch (fg). Inside: Library of Congress: Russell Lee: p. 14; Shutterstock: Bakdc: p. 33; Tono Balaguer: p. 31; Bird-Lee: p. 23; Diego G Diaz: p. 35; Manuela Durson: p. 1; Andrew Flavin: p. 25; Frontpage: p. 11; Martin Froyda: p. 6; John Gomez: p. 21; Mark Hayes: p. 20; Hikrcn: p. 19; Stephanie Kenner: p. 17; David Litman: p. 7; Mikeledray: pp. 12, 15; Page Light Studios: p. 10; Pespo: p. 41; Rickyd: pp. 4, 43; Christine Ruddy: p. 42; Saad315: p. 27; Savvapanf Photo: p. 29; James Steidl: p. 36; Chad Zuber: p. 26; U. S. Customs and Border Protection: pp. 8, 16, 37, 38, 40; U. S. Customs & Border Protection/Tim Tucciarone: pp. 9, 28; Wikimedia Commons: Official White House Photo by Shealah Craighead: p. 32; Pax Ahimsa Gethen: p. 30; Jerelconstantino: p. 22; Aaron "tango" Tang from Cambridge, MA, USA: p. 18; Dr. James Underhill: p. 13; U.S. Department of Homeland Security (DHS): p. 34.

Cataloging-in-Publication Data

Names: Croy, Anita.
Title: Border security: Are Immigrants Still Welcome in the United States? / Anita Croy.
Description: New York : Lucent Press, 2020. | Series: What's your viewpoint?
| Includes glossary and index.
Identifiers: ISBN 9781534565609 (pbk.) | ISBN 9781534565616 (library bound)
| ISBN 9781534565623 (ebook)
Subjects: LCSH: U.S. Border Patrol--Juvenile literature. | Border security--United States--Juvenile literature. | Border patrols--United States--Juvenile literature. | National security--United States--Juvenile literature.
Classification: LCC JV6483.C79 2020 | DDC 363.28'502373--dc23

Printed in the United States of America

CPSIA compliance information: Batch #BS19KL: For further information contact Greenhaven Publishing LLC, New York, New York at 1-844-317-7404.

Please visit our website, www.greenhavenpublishing.com. For a free color catalog of all our high-quality books, call toll free 1-844-317-7404 or fax 1-844-317-7405.

Contents

WHAT'S THE DEBATE?	4
CHAPTER ONE **BORDER SECURITY**	6
CHAPTER TWO **ILLEGAL IMMIGRATION**	12
CHAPTER THREE **THE TRAVEL BAN**	18
CHAPTER FOUR **THE BORDER WALL**	24
CHAPTER FIVE **THE DREAMERS**	30
CHAPTER SIX **DRUGS AND SMUGGLING**	36
BORDER SECURITY: WHAT'S NEXT?	42
THE FUTURE: WHAT'S YOUR VIEWPOINT?	44
Glossary	46
For More Information	47
Index	48

BORDER SECURITY

What's the Debate?

For decades, the United States has had open borders. Settlers arrived from Europe, Asia, Africa, and South and Central America. Some were looking for freedom to worship in their own way, and others were attracted by the opportunity to achieve economic success. However, many immigrants found life in the United States hard. By the late 1800s, some Americans had decided that newcomers threatened their lifestyles. The first limits on immigrants were introduced in 1875. In 1924, a new law limited all immigration. Variations on the law have been in existence ever since. However, there remains the challenge of just how a country with long land borders and coasts can prevent people from arriving illegally. In 2016, when he was campaigning for the presidency, Donald Trump identified illegal immigration and border security as key issues facing the United States.

This book looks at the debates surrounding border security. Read each chapter to find out about one debate. Then examine the ✔ and ✘ features at the end of the chapter, which explain both sides of the debate. Finally, review the "What's Your Viewpoint?" feature at the end of the chapter to make up your own mind about the debate. You can also find out what viewpoint people in leading positions hold by reading the "What's Their Viewpoint?" features. Let's start by taking a look at two arguments about the border.

A well-known saying about borders from the past is, "Strong fences make good neighbors."

WHAT'S THE DEBATE?

DEBATING BORDER SECURITY

FOR TIGHTER SECURITY

- The border with Mexico is a source of illegal immigration into the United States. It is also a major route for illegal drugs to enter the country.

- Some people feel that illegal immigrants take jobs from US workers and take advantage of education and social security.

- The wealth of the United States attracts many people from countries that are poorer or that lack civic freedoms.

- Better technology will make it easier to find and catch illegal immigrants inside the United States.

AGAINST TIGHTER SECURITY

- The United States has always offered a welcome to immigrants wanting a better life. Turning its back on such a tradition would be a betrayal of its values.

- Undocumented immigrants are a relatively small proportion of the population, and many have been here for years.

- Many immigrants make valuable contributions to the economy. Their labor is vital for the country's growth.

- The best way to tackle the drug problem is to educate Americans about drug abuse and thus destroy the market.

BORDER SECURITY

CHAPTER ONE
BORDER SECURITY

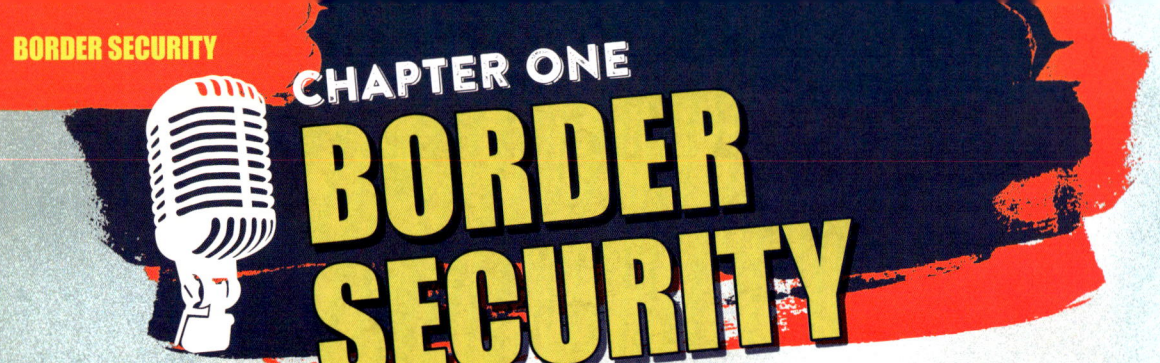

In the south, the United States shares a border 1,954 miles (3,145 km) long with Mexico. The border stretches from the Gulf of Mexico to the Pacific Ocean. In some places, the border is made up of natural barriers such as the Rio Grande. But in remote areas, the border is marked with only posts or signs. In the north, the border with Canada is 5,525 miles (8,892 km) long. It is the world's longest land boundary between two countries. Again, in some places, the border is lightly protected.

The United States also has long coasts on the Atlantic and Pacific oceans, including the Gulf of Mexico. Alaska has a shorter coast on the Arctic Ocean. In addition, there is US land around the world, such as Hawaii (a state) in the Pacific and Puerto Rico (a territory) in the Caribbean, that has its own shorter borders.

Debates, or discussions, about US border security are generally concerned with all these international borders. In fact, most of the debates tend to focus on the southwestern border with Mexico. Those who believe that the country needs more secure borders see this southern border as a gateway for illegal immigrants and for drug smuggling.

Much of the US border with Mexico is marked by a fence that is easily crossed.

Many immigrants take on jobs other workers are reluctant to do, such as seasonal agricultural labor.

Immigrants in the United States

Many of the debates about border security concern how to keep out illegal immigrants, and how to treat the 11–12 million illegal immigrants thought to be already in the United States. Many Americans acknowledge that illegal immigrants make a large contribution to the US economy. Opinion polls suggest some Americans believe such people should be allowed to become naturalized citizens of the United States.

However, many national and local politicians, and President Donald Trump himself, believe that such a move would encourage more illegal immigrants to try to enter the country. They fear that letting in too many foreigners will change the nature of the United States. They therefore think immigration should be limited. After he became president at the start of 2017, Trump argued that there was a direct link between illegal immigrants and crime within the United States. He called for increased border security as the only way to solve problems related to crime and drug addiction.

BORDER SECURITY

BORDER SECURITY

The Rise of Illegal Immigration

For most of the 1900s, Mexicans made up the majority of illegal immigrants to the United States. But toward the end of the century, many Central Americans also arrived. They hoped to have a chance to earn more money than at home.

A criminal business evolved in which people smugglers, known as "coyotes" or "polleros," charged migrants a fee to guide them across the border. The migrants paid when they arrived at their destination, which was usually a US city along the border. Other immigrants arrived legally on temporary visas, then stayed illegally among the larger Hispanic American community.

Hispanic Americans are one of the fastest-growing groups of people in the population. In 2015, for example, a survey estimated, or roughly figured out, that about 52.5 million Americans speak Spanish as their native language or speak Spanish and English equally. There are cities in the Southwest where Spanish speakers outnumber English speakers. Some Americans fear their culture is being "swamped." They call for stronger protection along the border.

The Border Patrol is one of the largest US law enforcement agencies. It has nearly 19,500 agents.

BORDER SECURITY

A new section of border wall is erected in California in June 2018. The sections are designed to be see-through.

A Border Wall

Donald Trump responded during his election campaign in 2016 by promising to build a "beautiful wall" all the way along the border with Mexico. The idea appealed to many of Trump's supporters, who see immigration as a serious problem, but other Americans were horrified. They were concerned at the cost of building a wall through empty desert. Many also argued that immigrants would simply find other ways into the country. Another objection concerned how building a wall might appear. Many Americans are proud of their country's reputation as one that welcomes immigrants. They worried that building a wall would send a signal that they wanted to be cut off from their neighbors.

WHAT'S THEIR VIEWPOINT?

Lee Francis Cissna became director of US Citizenship and Immigration Services in October 2017. That made him key to attempts to limit illegal immigration. In June 2018, Cissna announced that he was hiring dozens of attorneys and officials for his department. He wanted to target immigrants inside the United States who had gained their citizenship illegally by using false identities. He noted that more than 800 people granted citizenship had previously been deported under other names. He said, "We finally have a process in place to get to the bottom of all these bad cases and start denaturalizing people who should not have been naturalized in the first place."

BORDER SECURITY

Increased Threats

Among other threats that he believed were caused by immigration, Donald Trump highlighted the arrival of Muslims, who are often refugees fleeing violence or warfare. Trump and his supporters argued that some of these new arrivals followed radical forms of Islam that made them dislike the United States. Trump pointed to attacks by militant Islamists within the United States. He argued that the more Muslims entered the country, the more risk there was of similar attacks in the future.

As president, Trump proposed a temporary ban on all Muslims entering the United States. This would have affected nearly one-quarter of the world's population. Eventually, he banned immigrants from a group of mainly Muslim countries. The move was greeted with widespread protests. Critics argued that it broke the constitutional ban on discrimination based on religious grounds. The controversy was a reminder of the difficult balance for a nation such as the United States to achieve. It wants to protect its citizens, but it also wants to show that it is part of the wider world.

There are about 3.4 million Muslims in the United States. They make up about 1.1 percent of the US population.

BORDER SECURITY

✓ IMMIGRATION DAMAGES THE U.S.

David Stringer is a Republican state legislator from Arizona. In June 2018, he drew criticism when he said that he believed immigration threatened the country's way of life. He said that, if immigration was not quickly slowed, the country's "demographics" would be changed forever. Stringer was widely criticized for being racist, but stuck to his views.

✗ IMMIGRANTS HELP THE ECONOMY

Dennis E. Nixon is a banker in the border town of Laredo, Texas. In April 2018, *CNN* published that Nixon believed immigration allows us to benefit from a global economy and all the skills that immigrants bring with them. He felt we need new immigrants because there is, or could soon be, a "labor shortage" caused by a lack of people able to do particular jobs, fewer babies being born in the United States, and an "aging society" because people are living longer.

WHAT'S YOUR VIEWPOINT?

Do you agree with David Stringer's viewpoint, or that of Dennis Nixon? Use the prompts below to help form your viewpoint.

- Stringer warns that the United States is being changed by immigration Do you notice any evidence of this?
- Dennis Nixon sees immigration as part of belonging to a "global economy." How does a global economy benefit the United States?
- If there is a labor shortage, as Nixon predicts, what alternative ways might there be to fill jobs other than by encouraging immigration?

Cameras are one form of new technology being used to protect the border.

11

BORDER SECURITY

CHAPTER TWO
ILLEGAL IMMIGRATION

In 2016, about 1.2 million people became new permanent legal residents of the United States. About half of this number were new arrivals, and the others had already been living in the country. Polls suggest that, for many Americans, this is an acceptable level of immigration. It represents a less than 0.5 percent rise in the population.

The United States has often been called a "nation of immigrants." Apart from about 5.2 million Native Americans, who are 2 percent of the population, all the other 321 million Americans trace their families back to places other than the United States. Some people had no choice about becoming Americans. They included up to 500,000 black Africans shipped to the United States as slaves, who were the ancestors of today's 37 million African Americans. They also included Mexicans who became Americans when the United States took control of the Southwest in the mid-1800s. They were the ancestors of many of the 55 million Hispanic Americans, who make up about 17 percent of the U.S. population.

Some Americans feel threatened by illegal immigrants and want action taken against them.

12

Fear of Foreigners

Despite the close historical links between the United States and immigration, Americans have often been alarmed by the idea of large numbers of new arrivals. They feared American culture was under threat, or that immigrants might take jobs from US citizens. Foreigners have also often been suspected of introducing violent politics or terrorism into the country.

This kind of suspicion of foreigners is known as "nativism." It has been a feature of US politics for more than 160 years. In the second half of the 1800s, for example, nativists objected to the arrival of large numbers of Irish and Italians. Nativists mainly followed the Protestant form of Christianity. The newcomers were mainly Catholics. The nativists worried that they would change many parts of their families' lives in the United States.

These Chinese coal miners worked in Idaho Springs in the early 1900s.

The First Illegal Immigrants

Under pressure from nativists, the United States introduced its first limits on immigration in 1882. At the time, many Asians were arriving to help settle the West. The earliest regulations limited the number of Chinese who could settle in the country. Further immigration laws in the early 1900s also targeted mainly Asian settlers. After 1924, all new immigrants needed visas. The act also set limits on the number of immigrants arriving from specific countries, and put tighter border controls in place. After that, people who arrived in the United States without the correct documentation were considered "illegal immigrants."

BORDER SECURITY

Illegal Arrivals

After the 1924 Immigration Act, immigrants continued to arrive. They came mainly from Mexico, and later from Central America. These immigrants were welcomed as a source of cheap labor. When work was in short supply, the migrants were often sent back to Mexico. Some stayed in the United States, however. They had children or were joined by other members of their families, adding to the Hispanic American population.

Mexican farmworkers often helped harvest fruit and vegetable crops in the Southwest and Florida.

The peak of illegal immigration to the United States came in 2007. That year, there were an estimated 12.2 million illegal immigrants in the country, which was about 4 percent of the total population. From 2008, however, a financial crisis made work harder to find, and a significant number of illegal immigrants left the United States. By 2015, the total illegal population had fallen by more than 1 million and it continued to fall afterward.

It is difficult to collect reliable information about illegal immigrants. One estimate is more than half come from Mexico, and another 15 percent from Central America. The next-largest group comes from Asia, with smaller numbers from South America, the Caribbean, Europe, and Canada. Most illegal immigrants stay in the United States for more than 10 years.

ILLEGAL IMMIGRATION

A New Approach

In the 2016 presidential election, Donald Trump promised to stop people from coming into the country illegally. Trump blamed illegal immigrants for introducing crime to the United States, for smuggling drugs, and for taking jobs from Americans. Critics accused him of racism, but Trump's policies were popular enough for him to become president in January 2017. He called for an end to the practice of allowing people caught trying to enter the country to remain in the United States while their cases went to the courts. He also ordered US Immigration and Customs Enforcement (ICE) to increase its efforts to deport illegal immigrants already in the country.

Many Americans objected to breaking up families that had sometimes been settled members of communities for decades, and who had made contributions to the US economy. Some states and cities refused to carry out Trump's immigration policies. California offered sanctuary, or a safe place, to all illegal immigrants. Some cities declared themselves "sanctuary cities." They made little or no effort to deport illegal immigrants.

Donald Trump blamed illegal immigrants for bringing crime into the United States.

WHAT'S THEIR VIEWPOINT?

Haley Barbour is a former Republican governor of Mississippi. In July 2018, she wrote an article about immigration for *Time* magazine in which she said that people who had arrived in the United States without the correct documents but had since worked hard, paid their taxes, and been good citizens should be treated fairly. They should have to pay a fine and be put on probation for breaking immigration laws, then be allowed to apply for citizenship.

BORDER SECURITY

Cracking Down

In June 2018, the authorities began a move to limit illegal immigration that caused outrage. As part of a zero tolerance policy, they began to split up families caught crossing the border.

President Trump claimed that a trial of the zero tolerance approach had been successful, although experts questioned his figures. As part of the policy, adults caught crossing the border illegally are placed in federal jail to await a criminal trial. Children cannot stay in jail, so they have to be separated from their parents. The policy led to about 2,700 children being placed in detention centers. Images of families being separated, crying children, and the cages where some children were kept caused outrage among many Americans. Some complained that the policy went against traditional US sympathy for the young and innocent. Others said it was simply inhumane, or cruel. Even many Republicans made their opposition clear. The policy was quickly abandoned, but some families had still not been reunited months later. In addition, the authorities continued to insist that only zero tolerance would reduce the numbers of illegal immigrants.

Images of children being kept in cages and poor conditions made many Americans feel deeply uncomfortable.

ILLEGAL IMMIGRATION

✓ THE PARENTS ARE RESPONSIBLE

In June 2018, Attorney General Jeff Sessions defended the separation of families of illegal immigrants: "Noncitizens who cross our borders unlawfully, between our ports of entry, with children are not an exception. They are the ones who broke the law, they are the ones who endangered their own children on their trek. The United States, on the other hand, goes to extraordinary lengths to protect them while the parents go through a short detention period."

✗ THE GOVERNMENT IS AT FAULT

In June 2018, Laura Bush, a former First Lady, wrote an article in *The Washington Post*, in which she said that detained children should never be separated from their parents and that those already separated must be reunited immediately. She wrote that the policy was in conflict with the principles of the United States, which prides itself on being a moral nation that judges people on their character rather than their skin color.

WHAT'S YOUR VIEWPOINT?

Jeff Sessions and Laura Bush take opposing views about separating families. Consider these points to see which view you most agree with.

- Jeff Sessions says that parents have endangered their own children. Is there a way to punish parents that does not also punish their children?
- Laura Bush described the United States as a moral nation. In what ways might it be more or less moral than other countries?
- Jeff Sessions says families are only split up for a "short detention period." Does the length of that period make a difference in how you see the policy?

Many people agreed that children needed to be treated with kindness rather than harshness.

BORDER SECURITY

CHAPTER THREE
THE TRAVEL BAN

Donald Trump was elected president in 2016. He had promised to stop illegal immigration and to cut down on the numbers of legal immigrants. He blamed immigrants for reducing the number of jobs available to Americans and for raising the chances of terrorist attacks within the United States. He pointed to attacks on Americans within the United States that had been carried out by people from immigrant backgrounds.

In 2013, for example, three people died and more than 260 were injured when two brothers from Kyrgyzstan whose family was originally from the Russian republic of Chechnya detonated a bomb near the end of the Boston Marathon. The family had claimed asylum in the United States, and the brothers had become naturalized US citizens in 2012. They had become supporters of a radical form of Islam while in the United States.

First responders look after casualties following the bombing of the Boston Marathon in 2013.

THE TRAVEL BAN

Attack in San Bernardino

In 2015, a Pakistani-born terrorist named Tashfeen Malik, who was a permanent resident of the United States, carried out a mass shooting in San Bernardino, California, with her US-born husband, Syed Rizwan Farook. The couple attacked a workplace Christmas party, killing 14 people and seriously injuring 22 more. Again, the terrorists were acting in the cause of a radical form of Islam.

Donald Trump reacted to the San Bernardino attack by calling for a temporary, total ban on Muslims entering the United States. Trump repeated his call during his presidential election campaign. Critics said such a ban was unconstitutional, or illegal, because it discriminated against people on the grounds of religion. Trump changed his language. He called for a ban on immigrants from areas with a history of terrorism—but the majority of people in those countries were Muslim.

There are about 1.8 billion Muslims in the world, which is about 24 percent of the global population.

Soon after taking office in January 2017, President Trump signed Executive Order 13769. It banned all immigrants from seven countries—Iran, Iraq, Libya, Somalia, Sudan, Syria, and Yemen—but allowed in non-Muslims from those countries. It also lowered the number of refugees the United States would accept to 50,000, and halted the entry of all refugees from Syria. Many Syrians were trying to flee from Syria. A civil war was being fought there, and a terrorist group had taken control of large areas of the country.

BORDER SECURITY

Legal Challenges

Following Executive Order 13769, about 700 travelers were detained, or held, as they entered the United States. A further 60,000 visas were canceled so their holders could not travel. Many Americans objected to the ban. There were public protests, and critics called the ban "unconstitutional, un-American, and unlawful." The ban was suspended while it was reviewed by the courts.

In response, the White House issued Executive Order 13780. Its slightly different language suggested this was not a "Muslim ban." A ban on Muslims simply for being Muslims would be illegal under the Constitution because it discriminated against people on the grounds of their religion. The new order no longer allowed in religious minorities. It also provided for citizens from the countries involved to apply for a visa. Again, the order was challenged in the courts and was suspended.

In September 2017, President Trump issued Presidential Proclamation 9645. This version of the ban dropped Sudan from the list of banned countries, while adding Chad, North Korea, and Venezuela. Of these, only Chad has a Muslim majority. Although the ban was again challenged, the Supreme Court ruled in June 2018 that it was constitutional, and the ban was carried out.

The Constitution prohibits any legal restriction on the right to follow a particular religion, such as Islam.

THE TRAVEL BAN

Arguments Against the Ban

The arguments against the travel ban were both legal and political. The first legal challenge to the ban was that Donald Trump's own words about the ban in the past made it clear that the measure was aimed only at Muslims. That meant it was a form of religious discrimination, which is unconstitutional. Another legal argument against the ban was that it did not lie within the power of the president to introduce as an executive action. Instead, it should have been debated in Congress, like most new laws. Critics said that Trump did not have the authority to act in this way. He argued that the president has the right to take actions to protect the population. The Supreme Court ruled in the administration's favor by a close majority of five to four.

WHAT'S THEIR VIEWPOINT?

James R. Clapper was director of National Intelligence from 2010 to 2017. In April 2018, he and colleagues from the security services criticized the travel ban on the grounds that it was not constitutional and that it was unnecessary for targeting individual terrorists. He also argued that the ban would not reduce threats to the United States and might increase them. Clapper wrote that the ban would upset the governments of countries whose citizens were banned from entry. As a result, those countries might be unwilling to share information with the United States about genuine terrorist threats.

Donald Trump's opponents seized on the president's own description of the ban as an anti-Muslim measure.

BORDER SECURITY

Will the Ban Work?

A broader criticism of the travel ban was that it would not reduce terrorist attacks. Critics pointed out that no terrorist attacks in the United States have been carried out by citizens from any of the countries on the list. Countries that have been the source of terrorism, however, such as Saudi Arabia (which is where Osama bin Laden was born) did not appear on the list. There was also concern that the ban would cause resentment in Muslim countries, making them more hostile toward the United States.

Friends and relatives attend a memorial ceremony for victims killed in an incel terrorist attack in Isla Vista, California.

Some terrorism experts also argue that President Trump had chosen the wrong target. In terms of numbers, they argued, most people who carried out terrorist attacks in the United States were not Muslim immigrants at all. Instead, they were either American-born Muslims who could not be banned from their own country, or they were non-Muslims. A growing number of attacks, for example, are carried out by so-called incels, or "involuntary celibates." These are a group of single young men who resent women and normal society. From 2014 to late 2018, terrorists calling themselves incels carried out four mass shootings in the United States, killing 34 people.

THE TRAVEL BAN

✓ THE BAN WILL REDUCE TERRORISM

The Supreme Court ruled that the third version of the travel ban was legal in June 2018. They accepted government arguments that the ban was not directed against Muslims because of their religion. President Trump said in a statement: "The Supreme Court has upheld the clear authority of the President to defend the national security of the United States. In this era of worldwide terrorism and extremist movements bent on harming innocent civilians, we must properly vet those coming into our country."

✗ THE BAN WILL ONLY HELP TERRORISTS

In November 2017, 130 foreign policy experts criticized the travel ban. They wrote that it would damage relationships with countries that were helping the United States in the fight against terrorism. The ban also sent a message to those many Muslims around the world who are victims of Islamist terrorist groups, such as ISIS, that the United States really is—as claimed by ISIS—"at war with Islam."

Many people hoped the courts would outlaw the travel ban, but the third version of the law was judged to be legal.

WHAT'S YOUR VIEWPOINT?

Do you agree with Donald Trump or the foreign policy experts? Use the prompts below to help form your viewpoint.

- Donald Trump says that the president has the right to protect the security of the United States. Is a president the best judge of how to do that?
- The experts fear it appears that the United States is "at war with Islam." Is that a problem, if militant Islamists attack U.S. targets?
- President Trump wants to "vet" people visiting the country. How can border agents decide which visitors might be terrorists? What questions could they ask at the border?

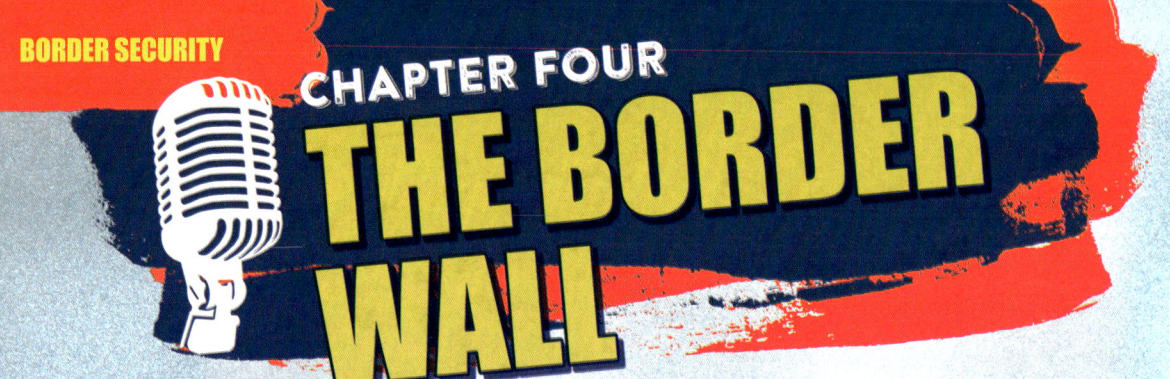

CHAPTER FOUR
THE BORDER WALL

During his campaign for president in 2016, one of Trump's main policies was a promise to build a wall along the US–Mexico border. He promised to force Mexico to pay for the wall. He said he would do this by taxing goods brought into the country from Mexico. He would also charge higher fees to Mexicans entering the United States. Later, he suggested that the wall could be covered in solar panels, which convert sunlight into electricity that could be sold to pay some of the costs of the wall.

When Trump announced in 2015 that he intended to run for US president, he highlighted illegal immigration from Mexico. He said, "When Mexico sends their people, they're not sending their best. They're not sending you. They're sending people that have lots of problems, and they're bringing those problems.... They're bringing drugs. They're bringing crime. They're rapists. And some, I assume, are good people." Many experts said this claim was inaccurate in its facts and racist in its attitudes.

The Border with Mexico

The United States land border with Mexico stretches 1,954 miles (3,145 km) from the Gulf of Mexico to the Pacific Ocean. Part of it runs along the course of the Rio Grande, but large parts of it run through desert. About one-third of the border has physical barriers in the form of fences or walls, and the border is patrolled by more than 20,000 agents of the Border Patrol. There are mountains and deserts on the border that are far less guarded, but these areas are dangerous. Up to 300 illegal immigrants die each year trying to cross the border. Far more are caught and returned to Mexico. Still, about 500,000 people cross the border illegally each year, usually in these remote regions.

THE BORDER WALL

In remote areas, the rugged landscape means that crossing the border can be very dangerous.

The Need for a Wall

Donald Trump argued that the only way to secure this border was by constructing a wall across it. About 640 miles (1,030 km) of fences already protect the border, following the Secure Fence Act of 2006. Trump described the current barriers as a "toy wall," although he also said that his intended "wall" could actually be a fence, as long as it worked.

Once he took office in January 2017, one of President Trump's first actions was to sign Executive Order 13767. It ordered work to begin on extending the barriers already in place along the border with Mexico. The Mexican president Enrique Peña Nieto repeatedly said that Mexico would not pay to build a new barrier. Nevertheless, construction of eight prototypes, or trial versions, of a border wall began at San Diego, California, in September 2017. In March 2018, Congress voted $1.6 billion for improved border security, including extending the existing barrier.

BORDER SECURITY

A Controversial Project

The wall was controversial for a number of reasons. Some people saw it as unnecessarily aggressive action toward a close neighbor, given what Trump had said about Mexico. They argued that Trump's arguments about Mexican "criminals" were factually inaccurate. Hispanic immigrants in fact have a lower crime rate than many other Americans. Other people believed that a wall would be too expensive to build.

Trump promised to build the wall relatively cheaply. His first estimate was that it would cost between $8 billion and $12 billion. Some observers argued that this was too little. The Department of Homeland Security estimated the cost at more than $21 billion. Other commentators believed it might rise far higher. Much of the wall would be built in remote, wild locations, raising the cost of construction. Building the wall would take about 3.5 years.

Mexican families in Tijuana visit with relatives living in the United States by meeting at the border fence.

THE BORDER WALL

The ocelot is among a number of species whose ranges might be disrupted by a border wall.

A Range of Objections

Numerous problems remain to be solved. People who own land along the border in places such as Texas have to allow the wall to be built. Some border states, such as California, object to the wall being built on their land. In addition, the barrier would divide the traditional homelands of Native Americans, such as some bands of Apaches. These groups are strongly opposed to such a barrier.

People concerned about nature have also raised objections to the wall. They say that a barrier would break up the territories of animals such as wildcats, ocelots, and jaguarundis. Vegetation would be cleared on either side of the barrier, further disrupting the migration of some types of butterflies. The route of the wall passes through a number of wildlife refuges, which are home to endangered, or threatened, animals such as the Mexican wolf and the Sonoran pronghorn, as well as a variety of plants.

WHAT'S THEIR VIEWPOINT?

In late 2016, Nelson Balido, chairman of the Border Commerce and Security Council, suggested that building a border wall would take too long. He proposed instead a "virtual wall" using the latest technology. He suggested that fiber-optic sensors and wireless communications could be used to support the Border Patrol's existing efforts at policing the border.

BORDER SECURITY

Will the Wall Be Built?

By early 2019, after Donald Trump had been in office for two years, it was still not clear if the border wall would be built. The trial sections of wall had been built, and part of the existing barriers near El Paso had been replaced by a new "bollard" style of wall made up of tall upright stakes. Congress had yet to approve funds for the whole project, however.

Although President Trump had promised that Mexico would pay for the wall, the Mexicans continued to reject the idea. Trump also referred to a report by the Center for Immigration Studies suggesting that the wall would actually save US taxpayers $64 billion in a decade. The report said the wall would lower the cost of welfare for illegal immigrants and reduce crime. Critics challenged the report's figures, however.

A continuing objection to the wall was simply that it would not work. Some people believed illegal immigrants will continue to find different ways to enter the United States. Others believed illegal immigration could be reduced more cheaply by improving the current system of border patrols, for example.

Many parts of the border already have walls or fences. Is it necessary to have a barrier along its whole length?

THE BORDER WALL

✓ THE WALL WILL MAKE A DIFFERENCE

Donald Trump believes a wall is necessary to protect the United States from illegal immigration and drugs. In March 2018, he said in a speech: "We started building our wall. I'm so proud of it. And we've already started.... I said, 'What a thing of beauty.' ... And we're getting that sucker built. The wall looks good. It's properly designed. That's what I do, I build. I was good at building, it was my best thing. Better than being president, I was good at building."

✗ A WALL WILL NOT SOLVE THE PROBLEM

Vicente Fox was president of Mexico from 2003 to 2006. In a January 2018 interview broadcast on the *CBSN* show *Red and Blue*, he rejected US plans for a border wall, saying that US taxpayers were free to make their own choices, but that he believed the wall would be a waste of money. He argued that there are smarter ways to secure the border and that, throughout history, walls, such as the Great Wall of China, have never worked.

WHAT'S YOUR VIEWPOINT?

Do you think a wall will make it easier to keep the border secure? Use the prompts below to form your viewpoint.

- Vicente Fox says it's up to Americans if they want to waste their money. Americans elected Donald Trump, so does that mean they have made up their minds about the wall?
- President Trump sees the wall as a construction project. In what ways could it be seen differently from other construction projects?
- Fox suggests the wall is not an intelligent way to secure the border. Can you think of better ways?

The United States has long been seen as a home for immigrants—but this makes some Americans concerned.

BORDER SECURITY

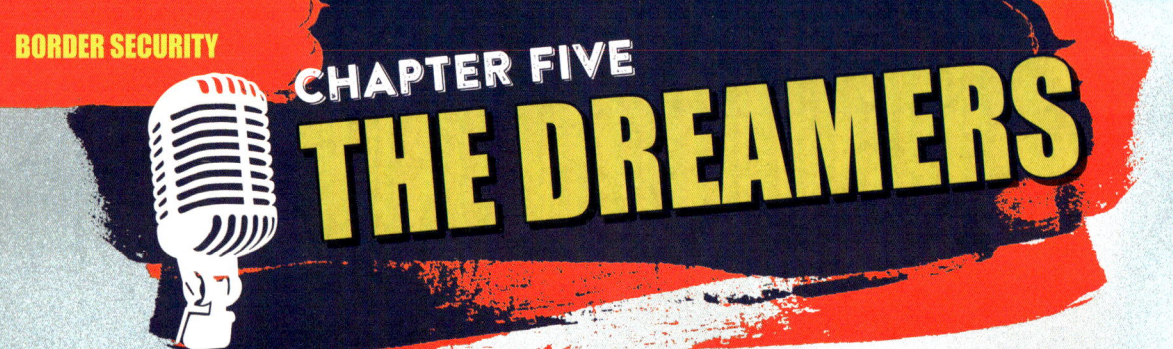

CHAPTER FIVE
THE DREAMERS

One of the most controversial aspects of immigration is the fate of the Dreamers. This is the name given to the children originally brought to the United States by parents who were illegal immigrants. In 2017, Donald Trump announced his intention to overturn legislation that granted such children special permission to stay in the United States. Many Americans took to the streets to protest his plan. However, action against the Dreamers remained limited because politicians disagreed about how to deal with them. Although the Dreamers were technically illegal immigrants, many Americans had sympathy for them. Most Dreamers had been brought to the United States without having any say in the decision.

Donald Trump's decision to cancel DACA (see opposite) brought large numbers of protesters onto the streets.

In early 2018, the Migration Policy Institute estimated that there were 3.6 million Dreamers in the United States. They take their name from the Development, Relief, and Education for Alien Minors Act, or DREAM Act, which was introduced to Congress in 2001 but has never been passed. About 800,000 of those young people had, however, been accepted into the Deferred Action on Childhood Arrivals program, known as DACA. (Deferred means delayed.) This program was created by former president Barack Obama in 2012, when he used a presidential action to order immigration authorities not to deport children of illegal immigrants.

Under the terms of DACA, recipients were given a period of deferred action on deportation. The deferral was renewable every two years, and only applied to recipients who passed background checks. Recipients also became eligible for a work permit in the United States. However, unlike the DREAM Act, DACA did not provide a path for its recipients to become US citizens. In 2014, Obama announced his intention to expand the program to cover more recent arrivals. A number of states challenged his decision, which was eventually blocked by the Supreme Court.

An Outpouring of Support

Supporters of both the DREAM Act and the DACA program argue that it is a basic principle of law that children should not be punished for the actions of their parents. When President Trump announced his decision to abandon the DACA program, there was widespread protest. Congress failed to come up with an alternative plan as Trump suggested. DACA survived its planned termination in March 2018 because its legal status was still being reviewed in the courts.

Politicians in Congress seemed unable to come up with a way to deal with the Dreamers.

BORDER SECURITY

Political Victims?

The possibility of offering the Dreamers a path to citizenship was considered by President Donald Trump. He suggested that he might go along with such a policy himself, but he also made it clear that his support would depend on Congress supporting other parts of his immigration policy. These included building a wall along the US–Mexico border, which the Democratic Party refused to support. By late 2018, any reform of the laws about the children of illegal immigrants had stalled in Congress. The deadlock, or lack of progress, between the Republicans and Democrats meant that the eventual fate of the Dreamers remained unknown.

President Trump (left) visits a school in Florida with a number of Dreamers among its students.

Congress could not agree on what, if anything, to put in the place of DACA or the DREAM Act. Some opponents of immigration proposed that the measures should simply be dropped altogether. The young people affected should be deported. For these critics, the fact that young people had not chosen to come to the United States did not alter the fact that they were illegal immigrants. Supporters of the Dreamers argued that it might be possible to create a new program that not only allowed them to stay in the country, but also offered them a chance to become legal US citizens.

32

Such a proposal angers opponents, who believe that it rewards illegal immigration. They argue that it would also encourage more illegal immigrants to try to enter the country with their own families.

Presidential Powers

In addition to believing DACA was wrong, President Trump argued that Obama's creation of the program had been illegal. Trump argued that Obama did not have the authority to create a program that altered US immigration policy, and that Obama had overreached his executive power. Although Obama and his supporters among the Democratic Party denied this, Trump's supporters argued that only Congress has the power to change immigration policy. However, Congress proved unable to come up with its own policy when it got the chance.

Supporters of the Dreamers argue that they should be allowed to become US citizens

WHAT'S THEIR VIEWPOINT?

Raúl Hinojosa-Ojeda is an expert on immigration and DACA at the University of California in Los Angeles (UCLA). In September 2017, he gave an interview that was published on the UCLA website. Hinojosa-Ojeda argued that, over 40 years, people eligible for DACA would contribute $3.6 trillion of economic activity to the US economy. Getting rid of them would cost the country workers whose education has already been paid for by US taxes. According to Hinojosa-Ojeda, the United States has benefited for decades from undocumented immigrants, but it offers no pathway for DACA recipients to achieve citizenship. He stated that rescinding DACA would not just do economic damage but also damage the "soul" of the country. It would mean turning its back on children who had grown up alongside us.

BORDER SECURITY

A Special Case?

Thousands of Americans took to the streets in protests throughout 2017 and 2018 to show their support for the Dreamers. Many of these protesters believe it is unfair to deport young people who have barely lived anywhere other than the United States. The average age of Dreamers is 26—and their average age when they entered the United States was six.

In addition, they point out that many Dreamers have shown themselves to be good "citizens." More than 97 percent of people on the DACA program are working or in school, including 900 who serve in the US military. Less than 1 percent have ever lost their status because of criminal activity or gang membership. For many Americans, these are exactly the kind of young people the country should be encouraging to become citizens.

Recipients of DACA meet in Washington, D.C., in 2016 to mark the four-year anniversary of the program.

A large number of Americans reject this argument. Their problem is often not the Dreamers themselves, but the message it would send to others if they were treated as a special case. Some of these people argue that there are established ways for immigrants to enter the country. The Dreamers should go "home," then apply to enter the United States in the same ways as any other immigrants. To give the Dreamers special treatment is unfair to other hopeful immigrants who have followed the rules.

THE DREAMERS

✓ MAKE AN ALLOWANCE FOR THE DREAMERS

John McCain was a Republican senator from Arizona. In September 2017, he discussed the Dreamers on *CNN*, including the 900 in the US military. He said that it was unthinkable to tell young people to go back to a country that they did not even know. He questioned how anyone could tell a soldier serving in Iraq or Afghanistan that they should go back to their birthplace.

✗ THROW THE DREAMERS OUT

Kris Kobach, an ally of President Trump, served as Kansas Secretary of State. In September 2017, he supported deporting recipients of DACA. He explained that, if they no longer had the status that President Obama had given them, they were "illegal." Therefore, they should go back to their country of birth, come to the United States legally, then become citizens.

WHAT'S YOUR VIEWPOINT?

McCain said it is wrong to send the Dreamers home, but Kobach says it's the right thing to do. Use these prompts to decide what you think.

- Is it possible to send a person to a homeland they have never visited? What problems might that cause?
- Kobach suggests Dreamers might be able to enter the country legally after they first return to their country of birth. Do you think that is fair?
- What do you think about McCain's reference to Dreamers who serve in the US military? Should military service earn illegal immigrants the right to become citizens?

Many Dreamers took the lead in protests against changes to their status.

BORDER SECURITY

CHAPTER SIX
DRUGS AND SMUGGLING

One of the biggest problems at the border is not immigration but smuggling, particularly of drugs. The Mexico border is the main gateway into the United States for illegal drugs, including marijuana, cocaine, and heroin. These drugs are smuggled across the border in various ways. They are often hidden in compartments in cars, or among goods carried on trucks. However, smugglers have also dug tunnels beneath the border to smuggle drugs. They sometimes use a catapult to shoot packages of drugs over the border for someone else to collect, or use boats to move the drugs from Mexico either up the West Coast or around the Gulf Coast to unload in the United States. In the last five years or so, drug trafficking, or transporting, has made more use of modern technology. Drugs are carried across the border by drones, or flying machines, or are dropped at sea in packages that give out a signal, allowing them to be located.

This border crossing in Tijuana is the busiest in the world. About 50,000 vehicles and 25,000 people on foot cross each day.

DRUGS AND SMUGGLING

One of the most common ways to smuggle drugs is to hide them in cars or trucks.

Mexico's Role

The trade is largely controlled by large criminal organizations in Mexico, known as cartels. Mexico itself is the source of the majority of illegal marijuana smuggled into the United States. (Nine US states and Washington, D.C., have made marijuana legal for adults. Another 30 states have made the drug legal if a physician says it is necessary for medical reasons.) It is also the main source of methamphetamine, a powerful drug made in laboratories on both sides of the border. The amount of heroin that comes from Mexico is also growing. Cocaine is often manufactured in Central America, but enters the United States via Mexico.

The Opioid Crisis

The United States has been trying to halt the flow of drugs into the country from Mexico for at least 50 years. This policy was known as the "war on drugs." In the early 2000s, however, preventing illegal drugs from entering the United States took on a new importance. The country was undergoing a crisis related to a class of drugs called opioids, which were based on the drug opium.

Many opioids are found in drugs used in medicine, such as painkillers. If people use them for too long, it can lead to addiction. This leads people to take stronger opioids, such as heroin and fentanyl, an artificial form of heroin. In 2016, taking opioids killed more than 42,000 people. The following year, the government said the situation was a public health emergency.

BORDER SECURITY

Crossing the Border

The amount of heroin seized by the US Border Patrol on the Mexico border tripled between 2009 and 2015. In 2015 alone, the amount of methamphetamine seized grew by nearly five times. In 2014, more than 500,000 people were arrested at the border for smuggling drugs.

Most drugs are smuggled through ports of entry, which are any legal places to enter the country. They are sold and used in small quantities that are easy to conceal. These drugs are hidden relatively easily in cars or boats, or in travelers' luggage. Some smugglers use "mules," or carriers, to transport the drugs, even by swallowing them in sealed packets. Unlike these "hard" drugs, marijuana tends to be smuggled between ports of entry. It is much bulkier and more difficult to conceal. Smugglers try to carry it over the border in remote regions, or even throw it over. President Trump suggested that falling bales of marijuana that had been thrown over the fence were a danger to Border Patrol agents, but most experts thought he was exaggerating to help make a point.

A Border Patrol helicopter flies above the Rio Grande to hunt for criminals smuggling drugs or people into the country.

DRUGS AND SMUGGLING

WHAT'S THEIR VIEWPOINT?

Sanho Tree of the Institute for Policy Studies is an expert in drug policies. In July 2017, *The Atlantic* magazine asked Tree what impact a border wall might have on drug smuggling from Mexico. Tree argued that the amount of drugs carried across the border was very small compared to those brought in other ways, such as through tunnels. He stated that the wall would do nothing to stop all the drugs that arrived through legal border checkpoints. Tree predicted that the drug problem might get worse. Dealers who are worried they might receive less heroin from Mexico would use an artificial version called fentanyl instead. Fentanyl is stronger than heroin, and potentially even more deadly.

Sophisticated Operation

Illegal drugs are a huge business. The Mexican cartels are thought to make between $19–$29 billion every year in the United States. They remain one step ahead of attempts to stop smuggling. They identify individuals who might take bribes, or payments for acting illegally. They go around, under, or over fences. They dig tunnels, or use fast boats to land drugs on the coast. They have come up with better ways to conceal drugs after the introduction of X-ray machines that can look inside vehicles at the border.

The cartels are also highly violent. Americans in states along the border fear the spread of violence from Mexico. More than 150,000 people have been killed in Mexico in disputes, or fights between cartels, and between the cartels and law enforcement agencies.

Other Goods

Drugs are not the only forbidden items smuggled across the border. Others include people, banned goods such as Cuban cigars, and stolen works of art. One of the most potentially damaging forms of smuggling is of fruits and vegetables. Plants or fruits can cause diseases that spread rapidly. In the late 1980s, a traveler carrying a diseased piece of fruit introduced Mediterranean fruit flies that caused billions of dollars of damage to the California fruit industry.

BORDER SECURITY

Is the Wall a Solution?

President Donald Trump suggested that one benefit of the wall he planned to build along the border with Mexico would be to prevent drugs from coming into the United States. However, many experts on drugs and drug policy do not believe the wall will have much impact on the flow of drugs into the country.

They point out that the majority of drugs enter through the 52 border crossings or via ports. In 2015, the Drug Enforcement Administration (DEA) reported that 95 percent of illegal drugs arrived in the United States in container ships and other vessels. The wall might even make the problem worse by taking money away from other efforts to stop drugs at the border.

For some experts, the problem is not the border but the high demand for drugs within the United States. The huge sums of money the cartels earn allow them to invest in technology to improve their smuggling and to bribe personnel in Mexico and the United States. Cutting off the flow of money is likely the best way to limit the power of the cartels.

Drug smugglers have built dozens of tunnels up to 875 yards (800 m) long beneath the border.

DRUGS AND SMUGGLING

✓ THE WALL WILL STOP DRUGS

In August 2017, President Donald Trump addressed a news conference and discussed the impact a border wall would have on drug smuggling: "Just to add on, tremendous drugs are pouring into the United States at levels that nobody has ever seen before. This has happened over the last three to four years in particular. The wall will stop much of the drugs from pouring into this country and poisoning our youth. We need the wall. It is imperative."

✗ THE WALL WILL NOT HELP

Alice Driver is a freelance journalist who specializes in US-Mexico border issues. In January 2018, she said in an article published by *CNN* that drug traffickers and people smugglers would be delighted if Trump built the wall because it would distract the United States from policing the border properly. Smugglers use the lastest technology, which cannot be stopped by a physical wall.

WHAT'S YOUR VIEWPOINT?

Trump believes his wall will work, but Alice Driver disagrees. Read these prompts and figure out your viewpoint on the issue.

Will a border wall help US relations with its neighbor—or drive them farther apart?

- Alice Driver says that dealers and traffickers would be delighted by Trump's plans for a wall. What do you think she means by that?
- Trump blames Mexico for the flow of illegal drugs into the United States. Would any barrier be able to prevent the flow of drugs altogether?
- Driver describes drug smuggling operations run on high technology. What high-tech solutions can you think of to get past a solid barrier such as a wall?

BORDER SECURITY

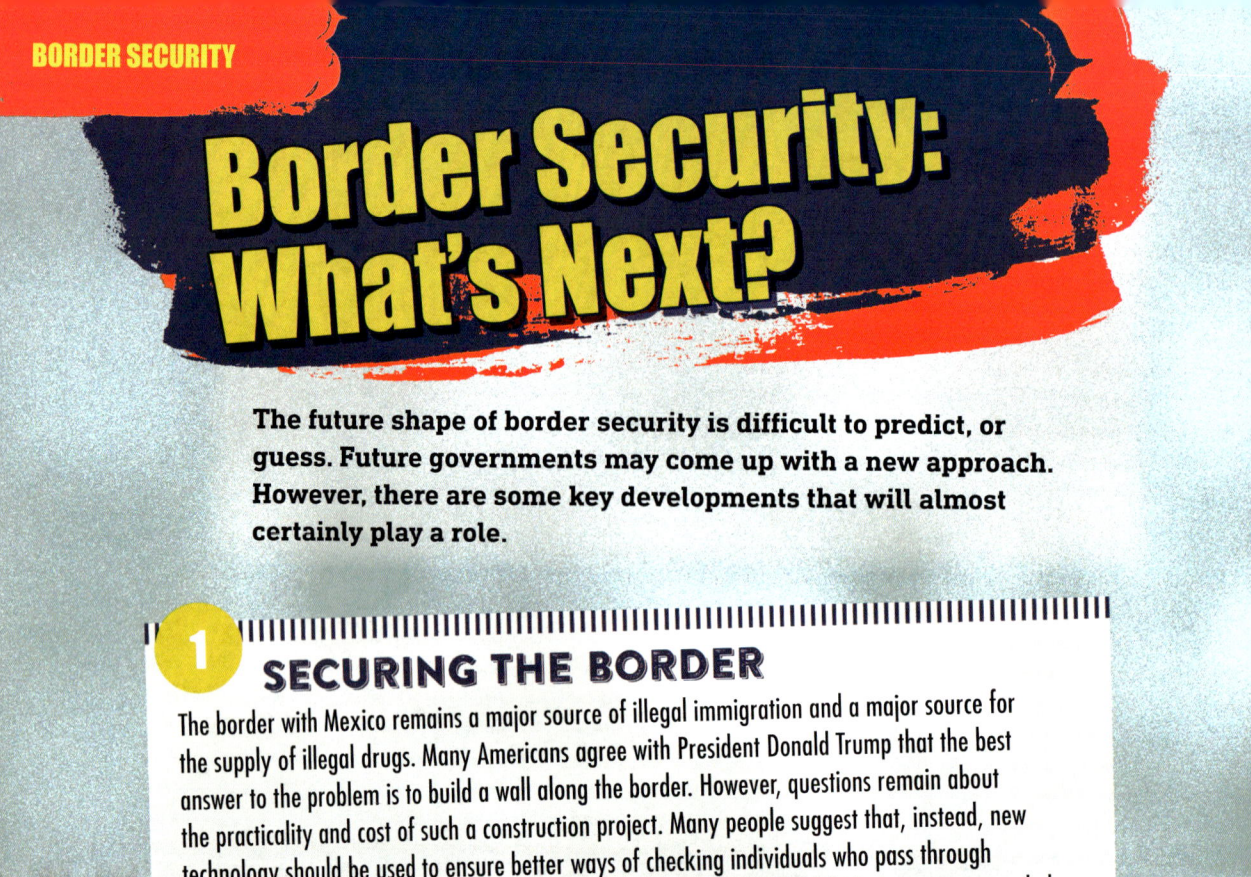

Border Security: What's Next?

The future shape of border security is difficult to predict, or guess. Future governments may come up with a new approach. However, there are some key developments that will almost certainly play a role.

1 SECURING THE BORDER

The border with Mexico remains a major source of illegal immigration and a major source for the supply of illegal drugs. Many Americans agree with President Donald Trump that the best answer to the problem is to build a wall along the border. However, questions remain about the practicality and cost of such a construction project. Many people suggest that, instead, new technology should be used to ensure better ways of checking individuals who pass through border crossings and better searches of cars, trucks, and other ways in which drugs are smuggled over the border or through ports.

This section of the border fence in Donna, Texas, has butterflies attached to it as a protest of President Trump's planned wall.

BORDER SECURITY: WHAT'S NEXT?

2 THE TRAVEL BAN

The travel ban introduced in 2018 was a reaction to the San Bernardino terrorist attack. Some experts claim it will only increase the risk of attack by offending many governments of Muslim-majority countries, which may lead to less international sharing of information about suspected terrorists. If this happens, US security services will need to step up their efforts to gain information from their equivalents in Islamic countries. Meanwhile, the United States is likely to have to deal with growing threats from terrorists living in the United States.

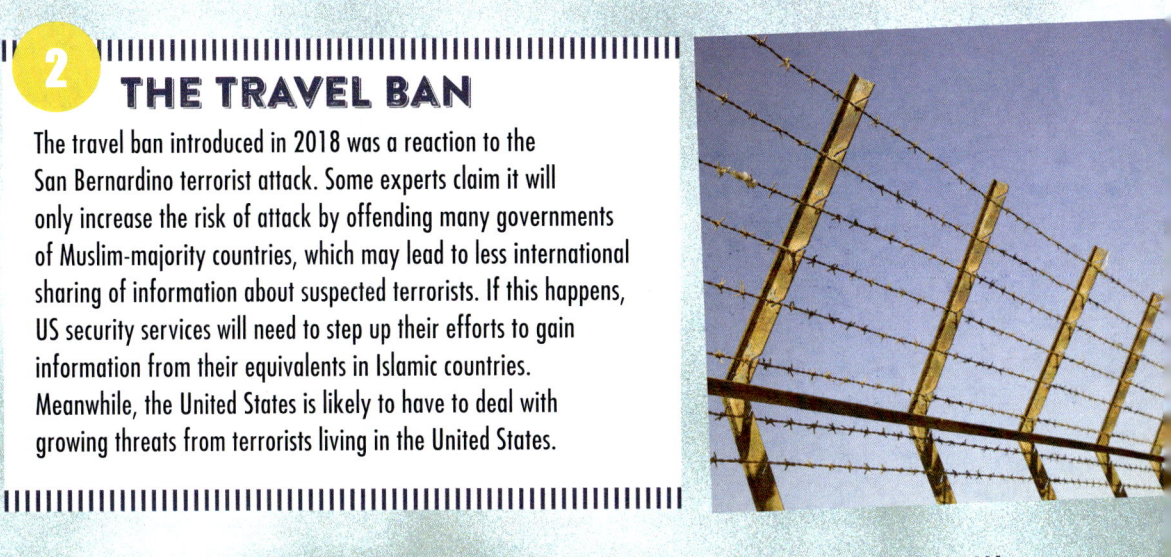

3 STOPPING ILLEGAL IMMIGRANTS

The US government introduced a zero tolerance policy toward illegal immigrants in 2018. It was a disaster, with upsetting images of distressed child immigrants being taken away from their parents. The policy was abandoned, and yet many people still believe that the system is too welcoming toward illegal immigrants. It seems likely that federal agencies will come up with a new policy that treats illegal immigrants harshly, but also ensures their human rights.

4 FATE OF THE DREAMERS

When President Trump questioned the status of DACA recipients and the larger community of Dreamers, he did so partly to begin a political debate on the issue. It seems likely that the president is happy to allow the Dreamers to remain in the United States, as long as in return he receives Democratic backing for building a border wall. This is unlikely to happen. In addition, many Republicans oppose making a special case of the Dreamers. As discussions continue in Congress, it is possible that the fates of 3.6 million US residents will remain uncertain for years.

BORDER SECURITY

The Future: What's Your Viewpoint?

Some observers are negative about the future of border security. Others are more positive. These expert viewpoints all predict possible future developments linked to subjects in this book. After reading this book, who do you think is right?

WHAT'S THEIR VIEWPOINT?

Joshua Tracy is a postgraduate student at Southern Methodist University in Dallas, Texas. He is an expert on the border region. In January 2018, he wrote that President Trump's border wall has many problems to overcome before it can be completed. Tracy hoped that Trump and his administration would think again about the whole project, questioning whether borders need protecting at all and whether walls are ever a sensible way of doing it. He noted that Former Arizona Governor and US Secretary of Homeland Security Secretary Janet Ann Napolitano once said, "Show me a 50-foot wall, and I'll show you a 51-foot ladder."

WHAT'S THEIR VIEWPOINT?

Julio Fuentes is the president of the Florida State Hispanic Chamber of Commerce. In early 2018, he told the *Miami Herald* that Florida knows about the benefits of the Dreamers better than most states, as there are more than 106,000 Floridians eligible for DACA. If Congress cannot reach a deal on their future, then 106,000 people would stop being part of Florida's economy, losing businesspeople, teachers, doctors, and serving soldiers. The state would also lose the economic benefits of all the businesses set up by Dreamers.

THE FUTURE: WHAT'S YOUR VIEWPOINT?

WHAT'S THEIR VIEWPOINT?

The Migration Policy Institute set up a task force to study immigration to the United States. Among the task force's recommendations were "accelerated implementation of 'smart border' measures that combine personnel, equipment, and technology to reduce illegal immigration and protect against terrorist entry." It also recommended strengthening security measures at legal points of entry, such as airports and seaports, and tightening the rules around issuing entry visas.

WHAT'S THEIR VIEWPOINT?

John Cassara is a former US Treasury special agent. He told the *Deseret News* in May 2017 that drugs are brought into the country by companies that have used complicated measures to hide who their owners are and who receives the money that they earn. He argued that a good way to fight against illegal drugs is to "follow the money" that is earned from their sale.

WHAT'S THEIR VIEWPOINT?

Shadi Hamid is an expert in US-Muslim relations at the Brookings Institution. In August 2018, he wrote about the Supreme Court's decision to uphold the travel ban. He said that, if people were upset by the Supreme Court's decision, the best way to express their moral judgement would be to vote against "anti-Muslim presidents" in future, and to persuade their fellow Americans to do the same.

WHAT'S YOUR VIEWPOINT?

The future of border security is complex. The viewpoints on these pages have supporters, but there are also many others. Even experts disagree about how best to secure the border, to prevent illegal immigration, and to stop the flow of drugs into the country. Use this book as a starting point to carry out your own research in books and online to develop your own viewpoint. Remember, there is no right or wrong answer—as long as you can justify your views.

Glossary

administration the government of a particular president
ancestors past relatives
asylum the safety offered by a state to someone who has been forced to leave their country as a refugee
bankrupting leaving someone broke
birthrate the number of babies born
cartel a group of suppliers of goods who cooperate to keep prices of goods artificially high
celibates people who do not marry or have sex
citizens legal residents of a country
citizenship the status of being a citizen
conscionable morally acceptable
constitutional allowed under the US Constitution
counterterrorism measures taken to prevent terrorist attacks
debates discussions of a topic in which different views are put forward
demographics statistical data relating to a population and groups within it
deport to expel a foreigner from a country
detained kept in custody
discrimination the unfair treatment of a group of people because of factors such as race or faith
effectively having a desired result
eligible having the right to something
enhancing improving
epidemic a rapid growth, spread, or development of something negative
exception different from everyone else
executive order a presidential decision that has the power of a law
fiber-optic glass or plastic fibers through which information is sent
global marketplace worldwide trade
immigration going to live permanently in another country
imperative absolutely necessary
intelligence military or political information
involuntary without choice
irrevocably unable to be undone
ISIS abbreviation for Islamic State in Iraq and Syria, a terrorist group
jeopardize endanger
militant Islamist someone who follows a strict interpretation of Islamic laws and is prepared to use violence to put those laws into practice
moral behaving in the right way
naturalized given citizenship of a new country
notion an idea or thought
novel unusual
policy a course of action
preemptively in advance
probation a trial period
racism a hatred of other races
radical extreme
rendered provided
rescinding canceling
robust strong
sensors devices that detect movement
smuggling illegally moving goods or people across a border
status position at a particular time
trade buying and selling goods and services
undocumented without official records
upheld supported
virtual wall a barrier created by electronic devices rather than a physical obstacle
visas official permissions to stay in a country for a set length of time
zero tolerance the strict application of the law with no exceptions

For More Information

BOOKS

Perritano, John. *Border Security* (On a Mission). Broomall, PA: Mason Crest, 2015.

Small, Cathleen. *Undocumented Immigrants* (Crossing the Border). New York, NY: Lucent Books, 2018.

Small, Cathleen. *U.S. Borders* (Crossing the Border). New York, NY: Lucent Books, 2018.

Staley, Erin. *I'm an Undocumented Immigrant. Now What?* (Teen Life 411). New York, NY: Rosen Young Adults, 2017.

WEBSITES

Border Wall *www.bbc.co.uk/news/resources/idt-d60acebe-2076-4bab-90b4-0e9a5f62ab12*
A page about the problems faced by the border wall.

Dreamers *www.theguardian.com/us-news/2017/sep/04/donald-trump-what-is-daca-dreamers*
Information about the Dreamers and DACA.

Drug Trafficking *drugabuse.com/library/drug-trafficking-statistics*
An article about how drugs are smuggled into the United States.

Immigration *people.howstuffworks.com/immigration.htm*
How immigration works, including illegal immigration.

Publisher's note to educators and parents: Our editors have carefully reviewed these websites to ensure that they are suitable for students. Many websites change frequently, however, and we cannot guarantee that a site's future contents will continue to meet our high standards of quality and educational value. Be advised that students should be closely supervised whenever they access the Internet.

Index

African Americans 12
Asians 13, 14

Balido, Nelson 27
Barbour, Haley 15
border length 6
Border Patrol 8, 24, 27, 38
border wall 9, 24–29, 32, 39, 40–41, 42, 43, 44
Boston Marathon bombing 18
Bush, Laura 17

cartels 37, 39, 40
Cassara, John 45
Catholics 13
children 15, 16, 17, 30–33, 43
Chinese immigrants 13
Cissna, Lee Francis 9
citizenship 9, 15, 31, 32, 33, 34, 35
Clapper, James R. 19
coastline 4, 6, 36, 39
Constitution 20
cost of wall 27
coyotes 8
crime 7, 8, 15, 24, 26, 28, 34, 37, 38, 41

DACA 30, 31, 32, 33, 34, 35, 43, 44
demographics, changing 11
deportation 15, 35
discrimination 10, 19, 45
DREAM Act 30, 31, 32, 33
Dreamers 30–33, 34–35, 43, 44
Driver, Alice 41
Drug Enforcement Agency (DEA) 40

drug smuggling 5, 6, 7, 36–39, 40–41, 42, 45

early settlers 4
executive orders 19, 20, 23, 25

Farook, Syed Rizwan 19
Fox, Vicente 29
Fuentes, Julio 44

Hamid, Shadi 45
Hinojosa-Ojeda, Raúl 33
Hispanic Americans 8, 12, 26

illegal immigration 4, 5, 6–9, 12–17, 18, 24, 27, 28–29, 30, 31, 32–33, 35, 42, 43, 45
Immigration Act 13, 14
Immigration and Customs Enforcement (ICE) 15
immigration limits 4, 7, 13
incels 22
intelligence-sharing 21, 43
ISIS 23
Islam 10, 18, 19, 20

Kobach, Kris 35

laborers 5, 7, 11, 14

Malik, Tashfeen 19
McCain, John 35
methamphetamine 37, 38
Mexicans 12, 14, 26
Mexico 5, 6, 24, 25, 29, 37
Migration Policy Institute 45
Muslims 10, 18, 19, 20, 21

Native Americans 12, 27

nativists 13
Nieto, Enrique Peña 25
Nixon, Dennis E. 11

opioid crisis 37

polleros 8
powers of the president 21, 33
probation 15

racism 11, 15, 24
San Bernardino attack 19
sanctuary cities 15
Secure Fence Act 25
separating families 15, 16, 17, 31
Sessions, Jeff 17
slaves 12
smuggling 5, 6, 7, 36–39, 40–41, 42
Stringer, David 11
Supreme Court rulings 18, 19, 20, 21, 23
Syrians 19

technologies 5, 11, 27, 41
terrorism 13, 18–19, 22, 23
tighter security 5, 13
Tracy, Joshua 44
travel ban 10, 18–23, 43
Tree, Sanho 39
Trump, President Donald 7, 9, 10, 15, 16, 19, 20–21, 22, 23, 24–31, 41, 42, 43
tunnels 40

visas 8, 13, 20, 28, 45

wildlife problems 27

zero tolerance 16, 43